TO TOUCH THE WATER

by
Gretel Ehrlich

Ahsahta Press

Boise State University
Boise, Idaho

Editor for Ahsahta Press: Tom Trusky

ISBN 0-916272-16-8

Library of Congress Catalog Card Number
80-69276

for
John Lewis Hopkin
and
all my Wyoming friends
whose Western hospitality
has been extravagant

Contents

Introduction

Gretel Ehrlich, film-maker, essayist, editor, cow-and-sheepherder, sophisticate of both coasts, when need be, and now, triumphantly, reborn poet—in the sense that poets of whatever age and reputation are reborn with better books, stronger poems than any done in the past—is a rarity: she writes poems not tailored to the needs of periodicals, East or West, or as steamy memos to an analyst, but out of the need to communicate, from time to time, with like spirits the fullness of her reality. It is a harsh one, even for one as giving as she, and only a very tough person—particularly if not born to it—could bear up to it, let alone, as is demonstrably clear in poem after poem in this collection, need it and love it to desperation. Harsh landscape, harsh weather, harsh work and, at times, harsh loving— that's her world, and she gives us good measure of it in these brave, sharply-imagined poems.

I like the poets who bear up to their worlds, and at their best ennoble it. I love the poets who do more than that, signal with *every* gesture, toward *every* humble thing making it up, their need for all of it. Gretel Ehrlich is of the latter group, as is seen in the remarkable *Other Seasons*, one stanza of which goes:

> You should hear the way snow
> sizzles and shrinks, hisses and rots away.
> Overnight someone new steps into
> those white thighs and drags herself downhill towards
> the next season.

Often she feels and observes fully, as throughout *Other Seasons*, sometimes very delicately, as in the lovely (save for the last unnecessary line of Part 5), very lovely *Six Songs to Tumbleweed*, the second part of which goes:

> Because of
> Tumbleweed . . . .
>
> Its small tangled woods
> Gone wild . . . .
>
> A storm
> Moves.

The poet's love poems are as full of storms, and they are among the strongest in the collection, particularly *A Way of Speaking*, which has densities of this kind:

> Once you showed me
> what time was by leaving me:
> when I forgot, you showed me again
> by coming back.

And there's the tender scroll-like ending of *A Sheepherder Named John*.

One could go on and on—as they say—, quoting powers and felicities, but more than most books I've seen, this needs little recommendation. The commitment to a full life in the toughest of worlds is here, everywhere, and so is the honesty and grace. I very much admire the spirit of this book, and feel, for what I know will be more than the moment, much enlarged by it. I hope so very much Gretel Ehrlich will make more important documentary films, write sensitive essays on Wyoming friends, tend all those sheep, lovingly, in one of the wildest, most thrilling landscapes anywhere; even when need be, leave it, so as to return with greater need. But more than any of that, I hope she will make more poems as strong and fine as those in **To Touch the Water**.

Lucien Stryk
DeKalb, Illinois
February, 1981

Probably She Is a River

Probably She Is a River

Probably she is a river where
seasonal mixtures run
rich: watercress, hot springs, ice floes stacked
in clerical collars on robes of
dark water folding and
unfolding around her.

Probably she lost track
of her reflection in the armed ambush
of willow stands.
She will not say her name.

Here is where
all the collisions of storms
fall out and swim home.

She rides those
hard boxcars with other
hoboes of winter: snowdrift, comet tail,
wounded deer.

Here, at the rapids,
she navigates her thin hips into surrenders.
Those strangers hunt and
touch and drink her longing to be invisible.

They do not fatten on it.

She loves them so she wants
to be their one predator.
They love her so they want her
wildness to be hunted in them.

They tow her on
thin train-floats of driftwood
into warm spots and out again past
bullet holes of rocks.

All her waters and liquors pulled this way.

Probably she cries out,
"I'm sinking."
Despite this vanity,
the river opens and accepts.

She is the water that carries her.

The Orchard

We go into it at night.
In Wyoming an orchard is the
only city around—so many blossoms going up
into trees like lights
and windfall apples like lives
coming down.

In the pickup, heads on the tailgate,
we lie on last year's hay and wait
for the orchard to bloom.
A great horned owl sweeps between
trees as if to cropdust the rising
sap with white for the flowers.

"The first blossom to come," you say,
"I'll give the apple that grows there to you."

Another owl lands
on a bare branch and drops
a plug of micebones to the roots.
Under him, the tree does not think of
the sap's struggle.
I listen to your heart. Divided by
beats and rests, it says yes, then no, then yes.

Above us the Milky Way seams the sky and is
stirred by a hand too big to see.
We watch the stars.

Tonight so many of them fall.

If You Wanted to Write a Poem

Think of yourself on
a great desert—like the Sahara—
with a good fast horse and
very little water.
You've been thirsty a long time.
Each time you talk
the thirst gets worse. You ride
quickly from
mirage to mirage
and each one has
real water.

Born in the Afternoon

for Victress Hitchcock

Against barbed wire an antelope
gives birth by the road. It's all sage here.
I drive through rings and rings of mountains.
The radio says: rain mixed with snow in the
southeast tonight; a traveler's advisory:
the mountain passes are slick.
In front of me a raincloud crowns the sky in
your direction, Vickie, where you're
breathing and birthing. Remember to stay in the moment
with the pain. Let this cloud draw rain
through your body to soothe and clean,
to nourish the child who's been growing there.
Right now earth gives two messages:
a female duck flies over the car;
the stub of a rainbow shoots up from
a ridge and disappears in clouds.
Child, Child, still unnamed, unsexed,
let go of your sleek garden of water,
lower yourself through the locks of your mother's body,
climb down this wet ladder of weather—
rain to earth—and wake up
on a pillow of sage where
antelope, too, are born in the afternoon.

In This Green Room

New York:
Your ferns stand against
mullioned windows. I water them
twice a week in slashed light
while you travel.

For five years
you have been in the
back of my throat like
laryngitis: nothing
about love said.

In this green room of
alphabets, venetian blinds carve
new words into shadow-bars and
jail your tongue.
Dismembered city light
moves over your jaw.
Inside, your white teeth have
a shark's honesty: too fierce,
they tear the frail tissue of
closeness apart.

We go out at night.
Unused to this vertiginous place
I sidestep from cliff-dwelling to
dry wash, my downhill feet
slipping into erosions.
We walk the length of Manhattan,
bleeding from the leech of lost love
and another time; love thought to be recovered,
turns leprous, eating into
the roughage of joined skin.

Now, halfway through
my thirties, the people I've loved
would fill this room.
And when tears come, they are
smaller eyes falling out of
my own, towards what they
can't see and what they can.

Other Seasons

Long flanks of snow straddled and
drifted my cabin all winter.
Held me the way a man would
if there had been one here.

If only I could drift into a place and
hold a time of year so elegantly.
Then break my legs leaving
to embrace the awkward spring decay.

You should hear the way snow
sizzles and shrinks, hisses and rots away.
Overnight someone new steps into
those white thighs and drags herself downhill towards

the next season. A thunderstorm
unties the sky. It composes and decomposes darkness,
and forgives what it has gathered there
by letting it rain.

Rain opens like a woman's shirt and
showers milk on corn.
A flood starts inside those ears,
a stranger's teeth drown in silk.

The rest of summer is
dust and under that, a thousand miles of
surface straight down.
Autumn comes

on bruised light, its knives and forks of
electricity carving sheets of rain.
Fall is breeding time. The bucks
are put in with the ewes

and under them dry grass
couples with snow.
Are we really
genetic or seasonal—dust to dust to dust—

everything skin-deep only?
This morning the last glass sill
of ice windowing the river
held what I am when I'm alone

but feel someone else
moving in me.

Six Songs

Six Songs to Tumbleweed

1.

Sea-fan.
Sweeper. Sieve of life.
Held breath.
Delicate one-foot.
Head that rolls.
Blow-up in my face . . . .

This sudden grass

Grace

Tumbleweed.

2.

Because of
Tumbleweed . . . .

Its small tangled woods
Gone wild . . . .

A storm
Moves.

3.

Tumbleweed travels
In wind
Gathering speed like a horse

Entering its last gait . . .
The mane rips out of
The neck. Fire fills

The arms
Of the rider.

4.

Clouds separate
Into waves of heat.
Eagle lifts off his steak dinner
Of hit-and-run rabbit, banks left
Over unclaimed land of
Pure calcium—White Mountains—

Tumbleweed flies beneath in
New snow.

5.

Tumbleweed stows away
On the undersides of trucks . . .

Tumbleweed sees the world.

6.

Tumbleweed lives on air.
Clouds point south in migratory patterns.
The wife of a cowboy burns
Last night's gathering of tumbleweeds to
Keep warm. Alone, she sings,
"This is my love, this is my love."
As it becomes winter, clouds
Heal together.
Tumbleweed is the last hair of earth.
Clouds fall through in the west as rain.
Tumbleweed sweeps up the light.

Two Songs

1. Summer

The blaze of tiny insects rubbing
their flash into luminous firefly wings.
The blaze of insect sex, the noise of it.
Serial bodies created whimsically,
the blaze of monotony.
The glare of snake serum
spreading inside your veins.
The blaze of black ash relighting itself from
past fires, the blaze of stacked irrigation pipes—
beginnings of bodies carrying water back and forth
across fields. The blaze of repetition.
Silvery fish-glint of silos and barntops,
matriarchs of these plains, the blaze
of yellow grasshearts, sudden boulders bumping up
under combines. The blaze of the blade.
The glare of an empty room as
you are leaving it, the afterlight of wheat,
the blaze of saliva emptied onto
small town pavement—strict markings. The blaze
of the branch-graft, point of incision blurred by
glint of sap.
The separate blazes of overlapping grass,
the glare of waxy fruit bubbling between leaves,
the glint of dry-hulled speedboats dragged
toward distant reservoirs, hundreds of miles away,
mirages of water softly shouldered in nearby hills.
The blaze of groundwinds slashing crops into
separate rows, cornsilk ablaze, blackening kernels.
Everything lonely to
the left of me and to the right—
this pastel of space growing
broader and higher in
thick suspensions of grass—the diction of flatland—
heat curving fields of it into whole mountains,
into the straw beds of
bottomless lakes.

2. Winter

Winter came
shaved by a river into
ground-clouds that lift
snow into the sky, into
steam that warms into
fog.

In the willow blur
her skin faded
the fade congealed as
ice afloat.

Under her
feet the broken
stones of the streambed
were new storms.

Portraits

Camilla

She was beautiful and she was broken down.
The wild sticks of her face were weights
that had begun to collapse and her skin was the last
dusty remnant of it. Her eyes were skylights on the scene.
The forms she made as sculptures were put there by architects.
Her father was one and her husband; she pulled them apart
and dilapidated them into anything but buildings—
wild places with no men.
Her hands shook. They shook into rainstorms, into
volcanoes that detonated her skin. It rained lava. Mountains
popped up made of clear unclimbable water. She was a painter
and painted all this beautifully.
In the rooms where she lived there were layers of glass,
weeds, cobwebs she would not break down, of dust, plastic
sheets, blue paint that swelled into more storms inside
her bed. There were leaks in the roof. Unruly hedges grew
inside the house. They were labyrinths that hid her.
She lived near the ocean. She unreeled swags of seaweed
into imaginary beings who made love to her while she grew
faint, went to seed, went soft by the passing of time with
no will.
On a friend's recommendation she ate liver. She drank. She lied.
She bit her husband's arm. She wept into the skylights of
her eyes until they were slits I could not see into.
The twigs of her face fell into her neck and were aqueducts
for her fears.
My own flights had unregistered blossoms, gestures recoiled
into bent-back hands. I could not touch down. She put hinges
on my heels and used me as a door to go into and out of
the braided branches she wore to keep warm.
She stayed in one place. I did all the moving until movement
no longer equated meaning for either of us.
I gave her all the turns and angles of my body and suggested
she build.
She drilled holes in the blood cliffs for adobe.
She planed the scrub forests smooth.
She took her husband back and her son and her father,

built a house inside herself for all of them and came
home to it.
The house was a hinge connected to earth through which
she would continually swing.

A Sheepherder's Binge

He rattles on ballbearings and spikes and mostly spikes
across the room.
He does the St. Vitus dance.
After a binge he can't walk the world flat.
His sleepwalker arms shake air in front of him with
staccato, off-center tilting.
He fights demons to get to the bathroom.
None of these tricks gives him bouyancy.
There are cuts on his face and feet.
In the rust of the pickup he hides his brain-scratches,
the suicidal loops, the terrible rusting liver.
He hides rust inside rust.
Brown whiskey, loose from the bottle, breaks into flames.
I swear, I saw him swallowing swords . . . .
His upper set of teeth spin out of his mouth as
he gags on the redundancy of family.
He goes back to the bars: the Cactus, the Medicine Wheel,
the Shoshone.
Now the gum-and-tongue gate passes only liquid. For two
weeks this goes on: whiskey in—vomit out.
Small town confidences dry heave him into a panic.
Passing cars lay a long slicker of slush against
his bowed legs as he weaves the streetloom,
braiding footsteps into tangled wants,
reversible conclusions.
Then he's through with it.
The batfaced woman who tends bar returns his teeth by mail.

Self-Portrait Through Four Ages, Four Phases of the Moon

The first time they cut her nails there was
a blackout in town. Then the sky filled with new moons.

As a child no one could explain to her how
that half-light on the breaks and draws of the earth
could come from so far away, and what was time if it was light,
and would she be old when the moon went down?

Later in her life she knew the moon. It rounded itself off
to a zero. A blackened nail on her hand rose over
the white sheets where she and a man who would die
were making love, and it eclipsed that perfection.

Long long after that knock-out
the moon came-to again.

Mansion

for Michael Mathers

I.

On the third floor above forty-nine
other other rooms, yours—the smallest of them all.
Wallpapered salmon, a monastic peach peeling at
every corner like a monk's robes unravelling—
He, like you, finally rebelling.
Skulls, spears from Africa, parts of animals' bodies,
books on existentialism, rows of masks, the diaries
of Thoreau and Emerson next to the double bed
where you sleep alone with a girl's name pencilled in
by the other pillow.
The long-faced windows search impeccable grounds
for a squirrel's cache, or for light, or for eyes
as lonely as yours to look into.
Summer squalls face off the heat, fall into
the green cups and slides of ivy and ride those steady vines
into your derelict room.

Up from her ovens of fresh-baked bread
your mother hangs horseshoe crabs over your dreaming head
and says, "Good luck, Mike. Become who you're afraid you're not."
For the rest of the morning you teeter over
the family fortunes: faultless collections of art,
ornithological displays, carved Buddhas who fold their legs
of space around the crowded opulence of rooms.

After lunch (you'd never skip a free meal), you hit
the road with a dime.
Explore then the people you might become: hoboes, sheepherders,
circus men, drag queens.
Examine the bodies of men and women—their fingerprint-proof
of uniqueness, every topographical curve you are not,
until at last you come to the part of this book of wonders
with the photographs.
Become what you are: an image-maker, a soul-snatcher.
Go play in those wide fields of light.

II.

Light.
Light scraped off the sunporch, the greenhouse, the servants'
quarters, off traintracks that led you west, off muted
steambath seductions, off pipes and posts and industrial parks,
off hobo jungles, off a bum's pint bottle tipped into the sun.
It all enters your solemn view camera.

Light scraped off the world's waters, the dead diamonds of
tides, off boat people, and the great polluted rivers—
all restored to the uncut light of your eye;
even the lesser lights wiped from your shoes,
until you are synonymous with light.

III.

Black is your appetite, your critical eye.
Your mother might as well have said, "Abandon hope.
Middle gray is enough."
Turn on your miner's light and descend. Shine it on
your own negativity.
Your mother might as well have said, "Be as bold in love
as you are in life."
Shine it into the passing trains you love. The open boxcar's
proscenium arch holds its scenes uncritically.
Be as bold as that.
Darkness is just another kind of light playing on things.
The train is a crossing path.
You cannot enter its rooms of love alone.

Tom Hudson, Pilot

In brown grass
seed covered with snow.
Hair travels through combs
as harvest: a life.

> *His boyishness was a spur*
> *floating from the heels of earth*
> *making curve-cuts*
> *in the bloat of air, marks of speed—*
> *and scars where speed was too great: a death.*

Autumn burns the body bright as leaf.

A Sheeprancher Named John

A swarming.
Orange as bees into hair, a face.
In a long overcoat of them he moves swiftly
by stings and grace across Big Horn Mountains,
against an upstream current of sheep.
When he speaks it is brutally to the point.
His fingers taper. A diamond ring orbits one of them
and is glazed by the silkdust of oats.
Orange, not direct light but
slanted, helplessly elegant, a color of
minor disrepute—faded chiffon draped
on the high, startled bones of his face.
Skin crisscrossed, uncertain tracks of aging,
irregular hems sewn, the threads pulled out.
His whole body, orange and burnt orange.
The abalone shell of his back with rich meat
under it, perfectly plumbed and moving sideways in
the sign of Cancer.
On his arms, sunspots like birdseed melted and
scraped smooth—burns on powdery skin.
How could it be so soft in a climate that weathers?
Mouth, a loose tear across the face, rarely
moved by shapes of words, but a listening apparatus—
lips slide apart, mark feelings awash and received.
Eyes are steady-state. Burnt all the way brown.
Shy penis, mostly
swirled white.

To Touch the Water

To Touch the Water

January: a simple operation on the heart of the earth.
Diagnose it: drought.
In a disguise of mothering
clouds cap off dry hills with male shadows:
no teats or womb.
A tractor moves on air, the whir of its seedless drills
floats above furrows, never touching earth.
The rancher who drives it is a generational skeleton,
dried back into his father and his father's father,
and all the way forward into his grandchildren's unborn bodies.

February: *to touch the water in your body.*
We've gotten the seasons mixed up.
I can't remember if I'm a man or a woman.
In the pine forest above us
branches are amputated from treetrunks,
splinter and condense into birdnests with no eggs.
Split cattails dry into swampbones.
Nightingales, meadowlarks, and red-tailed hawks dehydrate
in flight, grow thousands of brittle wings in their
flight over jack-knifed corn to find water.

March: the terror of fatigue.
Dust lunges up from plowed, unplanted fields
into gray panels of light
that search for the water in your body.

April: near
a dry waterhole two ducks
mate greedily. The gander locks his neck
down on hers and works himself in from the rear.

May: *to touch the water in your body.*
A dairy farm goes bankrupt.
The cows give out their last fevered milk.
What had once overflowed from buckets
is now the sky's white cataract
that cannot see we are dying of thirst.

June: *to touch the water in your body.*
Trees break off and dredge
dry earth like handplows.

July: thirst.
Twin Ponds is dry, Windy Point, Pond Twenty.
As we look for water
I know it's better that you can't read or
write well, that we are a compound of
bad tempers and silk flesh and
thoughts, unspoken, shuttled across our lips,
hieroglyphic.

August: *to touch the water in your body.*
In the pickup you let yourself down across
my chest. Eyes closed off by shyness.
Baled hay rises in
soft architectures around us.
Sheep bunch up and move out on
imaginary watercourses
creating eloquent and ambiguous geographies.
I lean against you.
I'm afraid of the deep learning
in your body which is bookless and
has no names for feelings.
Way back in May, all of Wyoming's water
channelled into your chest.
It's a vibrant stream richocheting inside you.
Give up your thirst,
the dry, unspoken affection.
Let me touch the water in your body.
The sky is filling with birds—
crows, magpies, eagles,
vultures—and they are
circling.

A Way of Speaking

Tonight is the one
that neither bosoms nor
spits us out, that cannot hatch
its eggs of desire or even
the ones that come after,
of nothingness.
Your hand does not go
around my breast to find
the milk there.
It was on this range we met,
moving your father's cattle.
We rode in dust. We laced our
strangers' lives behind the herd.
We did not know what kind of knot
we would make.
Standing in the stirrups at a dead run,
you showed me how to throw a loop and dally up
without losing fingers.
During the day our legs
touched, moved apart, touched again.
To live with cattle like we did
was to enter the inward blousing of grass
and drift there.
Once you showed me
what time was by leaving me;
when I forgot, you showed me again
by coming back.
That fall, on the Greybull River,
I saw how cowboys fish:
mounting a moss-slick rock
with high-heeled leaps, you hulked
over water.
You faced the current.
You dared trout to collide
with your too-big hook tied to bailing string
and when nothing bit you said,
"See, even fish think it's boring."

Once we entered that river.
It slit its neck so we
might use its voice.
Even so, I do not know if there is
a way of speaking that ever
takes one person to another,
or forward to what they might become.

A Hawk's Winter Landing

You call me one night and say,
"Better come on up here and keep me warm."
So I drive to the ranch.
Everywhere the white refrains of winter
carol out and out ahead of me.
Snowdrifts roll up and fall back from
the pickup until your house appears,
one planet of light
in this
Arctic sea.

At the door, you hold me.
It's like being gathered into
a nest of wishbones
all breaking in my favor.
"I love those mountains," you say,
the brim-sweat on your hat standing
in a halo of peaks around your head.
As I look at your face, your eyes
sew with tropical stitches
everything stark in me.

"It's a hard camp here," you warn me,
"Pipes froze, no heat,
nothing fancy in the way of food."
We go to a room.
As we undress, I dowse you
with haydust from morning,
those bright clippings scribbled fast
across your back as if to spell out
the emergency of being together,
the restraint we feel.

You get into bed
with your boots on.
I ask why. "Gal," you say,
"If I take them off,

I'll fall in love with you."
A draft in the room
roams us as if we belonged
to its spell, drifting and
banking over our two lives,
awkward on the swayback bed.

"Sweetheart," you say, "All these years . . ."
Outside snow begins to fall.
" . . . I've wanted you . . ."
It falls and is gathered in a willow's hairnet of frailty.
" . . . And now I'm afraid once I start . . ."
It spills on itself and sifts double.
" . . . I won't be able to stop . . ."
Against the house, trees rattling.
" . . . I'd like nothing better
than to die in your arms this way . . . ."

All night the drifts pull fans of white marriage rice
across us as if snow were beads of desire hurrying
to close the road. I say,
"If we are people on whom nothing is lost,
it only matters that we do not lose the night and who we are."
You turn to me. Even at forty, you're scared.
My hands go to your boots. I pull at the heels.
Your feet fly free. Your whole body floats up
like a hawk who might be lifting
out of a tree but is really landing.

For David

"What happens to people that love each other?"
"I suppose they have whatever they have and they are more fortunate
than others. Then one gets the emptiness forever."

Ernest Hemingway
Across the River and into the Trees

I.

Then we feed the cattle with
a sorrel team and a sled.
We break bales like bread
and scatter them before the wind.
Sometimes we cross the river
on bad ice to check for calves because
one cow backed up to a wash and
dropped her calf into the water.
And after, empty and light with no load,
we bump home across snowy furrows.

I dream we pull you
through all the seasons: through autumn's
hot temper when trees are
moods and the sky is
charcoaled black then whitestruck
until May. Then we are not
breaking bales but lives and they
are scattered bones in a crossing wind.

Sometimes I can't unharness you.
Your death is a horse.
I can't unwrap from my wrists these
leather lines that tie us together.
Then you lie in my lungs and
break words across my breath like water.
You tell me anything I can hear.

II.

Once when a surgeon said
your chances of making it were "pie in the sky,"
a mask of weather lowered over us.
I asked, "Ether or oxygen?" But the mask
just came down. That day broke you.
And when the clock unwound you said,
"Let's not tell time anymore."

III.

Now I have to learn words that say
the complication of who you were.
Memory breaks open its head and
throws you too far, then slams you close:
Eyes. Voice. Hands. Scar.
And the wind blows death into your black hair.

IV.

They buried your ashes and planted
a tree in them. Sometimes a wind
comes and shapes grass into
little bayonets as if protecting your absence.
And the tree, like the surgeon's needle,
punctures me with its spinal, bending song
until all the air is gone
from words and the emptiness I feel
is forever.

Cutting Wood On Shell Creek

We cut into dead bodies for heat.
Cottonwoods that stood up for
the first cattlemen in this valley
and pointed to water,
now firewood.
Dead too are your
grandfathers who bathed
and made children on this river,
then closed their eyes to
its surging brightness until
it spread forward to you.

When we use water in
Wyoming, we're using time.
Nine hours on a mountain
are metted out by simple
ablutions after love—
spring water, holy,
cupped over cockhead and face.

Even though I want to marry
you, be your sister-father-brother,
we can't adjust the river's
heretic clock of births, break-
ups and marriages to fit
who we are or learn
what water knows, that letting go
is real time, actual
passion whose
natural velocity mends
what is separate in the world.

Fourteen months gone by.
A skull's slow-moving
season of being "just friends"
hammered open. Inside:
your mind like a bee

stung by another bee—
fast, brooding, fiesty.
And in front of those
accordioned workings,
your eyes—trout-spotted,
sagging at far corners as if
pulled by some ancient
understanding of gravity—
that we are simply here.

Tonight Northern lights
shimmy up black poles and
shine, Kirilian, against
the Big Horn's false
scaffolding of permanence.
I've been flung to the dark
side of this planet and rise
as those black moons in your eyes,
swimming upstream in iris
towards the private
blue tenderness pulsing
there.

Irrigating Hayfields On the Shoshone River

The one thing I've
been retelling is water.
In sets of dreams water is turned,
the images by which we live
are tin dippered—water
drawn by hand.

Who can remember
what we are? As if
there had been
in any brackish pond
intentional ears of algae listening
not to what we've said,
but been.

A river is so fast to
leave the slush of snow in
summer, so fast
to be covered with ice,
so fast to cup
the spawn of trout and throw it
mid-river.

Downsteam is in sight
but out of reach.
Right now there are rapids.
Right now there is a
bend in the river where
muledeer drink and beavers
launch their wooden spans
like time across
what is always
leaving.

Ahsahta Press
MODERN AND CONTEMPORARY POETRY OF THE WEST

1975-76 (Modern series)

Selected Poems, by Norman Macleod
Selected Poems, by Gwendolen Haste
New & Selected Poems, by Peggy Pond Church

1976-77 (Contemporary series)

A Taste of the Knife, by Marnie Walsh
Headlands, Rising, by Robert Krieger
Winter Constellations, by Richard Blessing

1977-78 (Modern series)

My Seasons, by Haniel Long
Selected Poems, by H. L. Davis
Women Poets of the West: An Anthology

1978-79 (Contemporary series)

Stealing the Children, by Carolyne Wright
Songs, by Charley John Greasybear
Over DeSoto's Bones, by Conger Beasley, Jr.

1979-80 (Modern series)

The Hearkening Eye, by Hildegarde Flanner
To the Natural World, by Genevieve Taggard
Selected Poems, by Hazel Hall

1980-81 (Contemporary series)

No Moving Parts, by Susan Strayer Deal
To Touch the Water, by Gretel Ehrlich

AHSAHTA PRESS AT BOISE STATE UNIVERSITY
BOISE, IDAHO 83725